VELOCITY BANKING

STEP-BY-STEP GUIDE LIVING DEBT FREE

D1601501

By

CHARLIE NICHOLS

TABLE OF CONTENTS

Introduction

broke

adjective/brōk/

1. **having completely run out of money**.

We can all agree that being broke is NOT fun. Through the years, my meaning of "broke" has evolved. As a child, I felt broke when my only nickel got wedged in a Gumball machine (that required a quarter) in which my mom had to carry me kicking and screaming out of the store. As a young teen, being broke meant my allowance didn't cover a ticket to the movies. When I got my first job, broke meant my car running on fumes until payday. Broke in college was the Ramen Noodle Diet: breakfast, lunch and dinner (mostly because I spent my weekly food allowance on weekend beverages).

The real meaning of broke came when I moved out of my parent's home. That's when I first learned the phrase "paycheck-to-paycheck," and those utility companies really did turn off the lights or shut off the water if you didn't pay the bill on time. Even though my income was decent, my ignorance regarding finances began the unstable foundation for years (and years) to come. As my family grew, my financial problems not only magnified, but they also accelerated.

I'll admit, I was proud. I compared my family to others and struggled to keep up with those around me (anyone remember the Jones?). I wanted my children to have whatever their friends had. I began robbing Peter to pay Paul and when it was time to pay Peter back, that scoundrel Paul was nowhere to be found! Then like magic, equity loans and credit cards came to the rescue... or so I thought. My lack of financial intelligence, along with my glass-half-full mentality, began the slow agonizing fall of my financial demise. I danced, I dodged, I smiled, I wanted to give my children the world I thought they deserved. In the meantime, the debt grew out of control (who knew high interest and late payments could mount so quickly.) Long story short, I hit rock bottom... and hard. I'll spare you the details. If you're reading this book, you probably already know the details because you are living them.

My biggest regret, and the reason for writing this book, was while looking back, I struggled to find a single day in my adult life that debt wasn't at the forefront of my mind. On the outside, I was smiling, laughing, and playing the part of the happy middle-class mom, while on the inside, I was trapped in worry and constantly crunching the numbers. Debt had robbed me of being more...not only for my children, but also to everyone around me. There is no such thing as "living in the moment" with a dark cloud of debt looming just above your head.

As much as I did NOT want that same life for my children, I began to see familiar patterns in their attitudes and views regarding money. Sadly, I realized I had not provided them with the rules to win the "real life" game of Monopoly, obviously because I had never had them myself. I looked around me and noticed everyone I knew (friends, co-workers, family, people I met in line at the grocery store) all seemed to share the same struggle; trading time for money, living paycheck-to-paycheck, and slowly slipping into a debt trap.

Was *everyone* playing with the wrong set of rules? I had enough. I began my search to find an answer.

Word of Caution: The Velocity Banking strategy will not work for everyone. I am not trying to sell anyone on the concept. Because Velocity Banking worked (and continues to work) for me, I thought it might be helpful to share my experiences with those who find themselves in similar circumstances. Especially those who have a hard time saving or that have no savings at all. You know yourself better than anyone else, and if you cannot trust yourself with credit, and hate crunching numbers, this strategy is not for you. It is a numbers game, and you need to stay on top of your monthly statements to be successful. There are many different strategies out there for tackling debt, and maybe one of those would be more suited to your needs.

Chapter 1

It's Payday!

Most of us, who trade our time for money, either have our paychecks loaded onto an employee's debit card, or directly deposited into a checking account. From there, we pay our bills and monthly living expenses. At the end of the month, any leftover funds (if we are lucky) get transferred into some type of savings account. This has been the accepted way of handling personal finances for generations. When I received my first paycheck, my parents were quick to take me down to the local bank and assisted me in opening my first accounts. I can still remember how excited I was to receive that box of checks. *I was finally a grown up!* Each time I received a paycheck, my parents offered their advice on the amount I should be depositing into my checking and to make sure I was saving for a "rainy day." That was my introduction to the banking system I used for decades... the same system used by most working individuals today.

Banks have strategically, and successfully, led us to believe these accounts are necessary to properly manage our family finances. In the past they offered you small appliances, a toaster or maybe a blender, if you opened an account with them. Today they offer you cash, sometimes as much as $500 for signing up for a direct deposit or savings account. I have seen offers as high as $750 if you refer someone else to sign up. As soon as you become a part of their "family," you will be inundated with an array of offers for banking and loan products. Who do you suppose benefits the most from the financial "conveniences" they advertise? Well, let's follow the money.

Fees and Charges

A recent study by Bank Fee Finder Report found that, last year, the average American spent $329 on bank fees. Three-hundred-twenty-nine dollars!

Furthermore, the average bank account monthly maintenance fee is more than $13 a month. That means $156 a year, just for having an account.

ATM fees are up and they're probably going to get worse.

Additional bank fees can include:

Monthly account fee

Minimum balance fee

Overdraft/NSF fee

Overdraft protection fee

Return deposit fee

Additional checks fee

Cashier check fee

Paper statement fee

ATM fee

Debit card transfer fee

Lost card fee

Foreign transaction fee

Wire transfer fee

Savings withdrawal fee (after the six-in-a-month limit)

What you should be paying is zero dollars. Imagine someone making you this offer, "Excuse me, consumer, will you give me your money? I'll hold onto it for you, invest it and make tons of money from it, but not share any of that profit with you. And in return you can have it back, with a pittance of interest and minus the fees, of course."

Sounds outrageous, right? Yet, year after year, people pay hundreds or even thousands of dollars in bank fees. And who is paying the most? Low-income people. Not surprisingly, the people with the least money end up paying the most for owning a bank account. The Consumer Financial Protection Bureau found that just 9% of people pay 80% of all bank fees and they're mostly on the lower end of the income scale. Low-income consumers pay $522 a year in fees for checking accounts.

Fractional Reserve Banking

Most people have never heard of "Fractional Reserve Banking." The federal reserve only requires banks to keep 10% of their customers' deposits, referred to as reserves. That leaves 90% available for them to loan back to other parties (with interest), sometimes even back to you, yourself; when you finance that new car, apply for a line of credit or maybe your first mortgage. Another interesting note, the federal reserve pays the banks interest on whatever deposits they keep in reserves. On our money! Banks are not just there for our convenience as they have led us to believe. Like any other business, they are there to make money... big money. And, making money is fine, it's the American way. We just need to educate ourselves so that we are on a level playing field with the banking industry. If we are getting ripped off by financial institutions, it is most likely due to our own financial ignorance.

Outdated System

What I am about to suggest will most likely raise some brows, but... here goes. This system of banking is inefficient, outdated, and was set up by big banks to keep the little guy living paycheck-to-paycheck. Checking and savings accounts serve *no* purpose from a monetary standpoint, other than liquidity. Banks pay you a pittance, if any, to park your money to sit idle, while charging "you" fees and, in turn, make millions of dollars by loaning that same money back out with hefty interest rates attached. I bet you didn't realize how hard your money was working... it is, just not for you.

Your Income Should Have an Impact

Every dollar you earn should have a purpose and a positive impact. The four things your income should be accomplishing:

1) **Cancel Interest:** If you have high-interest debt, this is what your income should be doing first.

2) **Make Interest:** Your income should be earning you more income through investments.

3) **Pay Expenses:** You must pay your bills.

4) **Build Wealth:** Your money should build your wealth through some sort of investment plan or passive income.

The problem is, for most people who find themselves on the debt hamster wheel, are only doing one of these, paying expenses.

Chapter 2

Drowning in Debt

According to the Federal Reserve, the average American household carries $38,000 in non-mortgage debt. Whether it be credit cards, student loans, medical bills, payday loans, or vehicle loans, most Americans have some combination of these sources of debt. Families are struggling to stay afloat. Most people are working harder than ever (again, trading time for money), sometimes at two or more jobs, just to be able to afford the minimum payments, which are not only padded in interest, but also increasing the amount of time to pay them off.

One-income families have become a thing of the past. It now takes two incomes (full-time) just to keep just to keep us above, or hoovering close to, the poverty level in many parts of the country.

Consumer debt is our number one enemy. It has paralyzed us as a nation. We have put ourselves into such debt arrangements with no savings to fall back on. A recent Federal Reserve Economic report noted that 40% of adults in the United States do not have enough money in their savings to cover an unexpected $400 expense. Those who don't have the cash on hand say they'd have to cover an emergency by borrowing or selling something.

Debt is often a taboo subject that most people hide from their family and friends. The seclusion and guilt of struggling financially often leads to anxiety and depression. According to a study by the American Psychological Association, people dealing with debt are also more likely to report health problems. The stress of being in debt is a harrowing experience and affects all areas of an individual's life, as well as their family. Arguments over money still reign high on the list of causes for divorce between married couples. It is impossible to live in the "moment," which we are told is the *key to happiness* when we are constantly worrying about debt.

Even though the statistics paint a dire picture of debt in America, it's important to understand that not *all* debt is bad. Robert Kiyosaki, the author of the Rich Dad, Poor Dad books, teaches that debt can be used to our advantage. Kiyosaki built his riches using other people's money (OPM). He explains the difference between "good debt" (putting money in your pocket) and "bad debt" (taking money out of your pocket). Wealthy people understand this difference and only use debt (good debt) to purchase income-producing assets that increase their cash flow. Those of us who struggle financially tend to use debt (bad debt) to purchase liabilities; for instance, the latest cell phone, big screen televisions, vehicles, vacations, or anything else that will essentially take money from our pockets. Understanding the difference between good debt and bad debt is one of the first steps toward living a financially independent life.

Finding the Answer

We have all heard the financial gurus shouting their mantras: "Cut up your cards, start an emergency fund, get a second job, ride your bike, embrace the Ramen Noodle diet, sell your kids... In theory, this "slap-in-the-face" advice should work, but *only* if you are able to follow the strict rules required while severely altering your lifestyle. I, myself, have read several of these authors' books and picked up many great tips and advice regarding personal finances and debt reduction. Each time I finished a book, I would be extremely motivated to tackle my debt, only to "fall off the wagon" after a few pay cycles. The changes they demanded were just too difficult for me to maintain. After each relapse, I would feel like a total failure; the books sitting on my desk (under a stack of bills), scolding me like a naughty child: "Bad consumer, bad, bad consumer!"

Of course, we need to take responsibility for the financial positions we are in, but even more important is to understand how and why we arrived at this point, to begin with.

We repeat what we know so right out of the gate we are pretty much doomed to follow a life filled with trading time for money. We are indoctrinated from an early age as to what a successful life should look like. I don't believe our parents are aware of the damage caused by passing along the same "map" of success that was passed on to them. No one questions the map, so the cycle goes on.

We have all followed it: Finish your education, get a good job, buy a nice vehicle, buy a house and furnishings, get married, have a child, second vehicle, put in a pool for the kids, a hot tub, have a second child, take a family vacation. Now that is success!

But behind that pretty picture: Student loan payments, trading of time, vehicle payment, mortgage payment, credit card interest (furnishings, engagement ring, wedding expenses), growing family needs, increased insurance, second vehicle payment, second mortgage for pool and hot tub, more interest on credit card carry over, vacation expenses.

Chapter 3

Good News! There's a Better Way

During my search to find a debt reduction plan I could realistically follow, I kept coming across the term "velocity banking". The strategy was being used as a tool for people that have a hard time saving money or have nothing saved in the first place. Bingo! It quickly got my attention.

The debt reduction strategy was unlike anything I had come across before. Although a bit skeptical, I found myself intrigued enough to continue researching. The concept of using credit to pay off debt went against everything I had ever been taught. Of course, everything I had been taught about money and finance came from the banks. Paying off debt with credit cards? Sounds crazy, huh? But people were doing it and doing it successfully.

The main vehicle used in velocity banking is an interest-bearing account that remains liquid. A line of credit (LOC) is the tool used for this task. With a LOC, we are charged interest on the average daily balance, but we can put our money in and take it back out to use over and over again. Another very important thing to mention is that this is referred to as using the bank's money or other people's money (OPM).

People using the velocity banking strategy (sometimes called *Paycheck Parking* or *Chunking*) are reportedly paying off high-interest credit cards and student loans at a rapid pace. Homeowners were saving thousands in interest by using the method to pay off 30-year mortgages in 5-7 years! Paying off my mortgage quickly was certainly a goal of mine, but I first had to tackle my credit cards and student loans.

The more I learned about velocity banking, along with its many success stories, the more I was convinced the strategy would work for me. It was different from anything I had tried before. First, because I would be able to use my current income, and second, I wouldn't have to sacrifice my lifestyle. So, what was there to lose?

The only requirements for velocity banking were to have a line of credit (for me, my credit card) and to have at least $500 left over after paying the monthly expenses (cash flow). At the time I had approximately $400 left over each month. I knew if I tried hard enough, I could come up with an additional $100 in cash flow. I will explain how I was able to accomplish this later.

Benefits of the Velocity Banking

1) Velocity banking can be leveraged to make a payment towards a bad loan, or even as a down payment on an investment. It works as a great tool because you only pay interest on the money you are currently using.

2) Velocity banking decreases debt rapidly.

Whether it be credit card debt, student loans, car loans, payday loans, or mortgages, they all can be targeted using velocity banking.

3) Velocity banking increases the principal paid.

Because more money is paid to the principle (chunking), thus, canceling out the interest. (This is not an extra payment type strategy).

4) Velocity banking increases FICO scores.

As your balances decrease so does your debt-to-income ratios.

5) Velocity banking increases monthly cash flow.

You will free up cash as your debt obligations decrease.

6) Velocity banking increases cash availability.

You will have access to more cash. Think of it as your old emergency or rainy-day fund. Velocity banking allows you to have access to cash by using revolving credit.

7) Velocity banking requires no approval.

Because you are using a LOC, you do not need an approval to use the money; you can go online and quickly transfer money wherever it needs to go.

8) Velocity banking creates financial independence.

Once your debt is wiped out, and you have learned how to leverage debt (banks money), you can use it as a vehicle to grow wealth... financial independence.

9) Velocity banking reduces stress.

You will finally feel in control when you can see your money working for you and your goals.

So Why Aren't More People Using This?

You will not hear about "velocity banking" from banks, for obvious reasons. Banks want to sell products that benefit themselves... period.

The media don't understand it. Velocity banking is not difficult to learn; however, it does go against our way of thinking about how we are supposed to do banking. Thus, making it a little complicated and confusing at first.

Many financial advisors have never heard of it. Again, we live in a society that always follows traditions, and people do *not* like change. Our financial advisors are in the same situation and are taught by the same schools.

Lastly, our grandparents and parents never did it. They passed down their (well-intentioned) beliefs regarding money; just as mine did when they proudly walked me into their bank to open my first checking and savings account. So, if your parents never did this, you probably didn't either.

I received a lot of resistance whenever I tried explaining the velocity banking concept to others. Whether it be to friends or family, everyone seemed to be a financial expert (although, none had a handle on their own finances). Because I understood the concept, through researching with an "open mind," I believed it was right for me and the proof was going to have to be in the pudding.

Word of Caution: The velocity banking strategy will not work for everyone. I am not trying to sell anyone on the concept. Because velocity banking worked (and continues to work) for me, I thought it might be helpful for others who find themselves searching for strategies to rapidly eliminate debt. Especially those who have a hard time saving or that have no savings at all. You know yourself better than anyone else, and if you cannot trust yourself with credit, and hate crunching numbers, this strategy is not for you. It is a numbers game, and you need to stay on top of your monthly statements to be successful. There are many different strategies out there for tackling debt, and maybe one of those would be more suited to your needs.

Chapter 4

Creating the Velocity Banking System

1) Assess Your Current Situation – Monthly Tracker Form

The first step in creating your debt reduction plan is... you guessed it, tracking your spending. It is the most critical step toward eliminating debt. Believe me, you will be amazed when you finally sit down and get serious as to what is going on with your finances, and that means accounting for *everything*. This must be honest accounting. Don't just try to guess or fudge the numbers because you think they won't make a difference. Every penny counts! Besides, you traded the world's most precious asset for your pennies...your time.

Tracking my spending made me feel as if I was finally taking control of something that had controlled me most of my adult life. I eagerly accounted for every penny for an entire month. I felt liberated during the process, and sometimes foolish when I discovered where my hard-earned income was going (money I was trading my time for). At least, it gave me the answer to the age-old question "where does it all go?"

2) Calculating Your Monthly Cash flow—Monthly Income/Expense Form

Now that you have an accurate accounting of your discretionary spending, you will be able to calculate your cash flow with the Monthly Income/Expense Statement. For velocity banking to work your income must be greater than your monthly expenses (income - expenses = cash flow). This may sound obvious, but a lot of people are surprised once they take a hard look at their numbers. Maybe your cash flow is more than you thought, but most likely it will be less. For velocity banking to be successful, you should aim for a cash flow of at least $500.

Do not despair if you are not there yet. As I stated earlier, when I first created my Monthly Income/Expense Statement, my cash flow was about $400 a month. Once I had a better understanding of where my money was going, I quickly saw the "holes I could plug," the first being my coffee breaks to McDonald's. I was spending on average, $3.20 for an iced frappe at least 5-days-a-week, with an occasional $5 Carmel Marvel from Bigby thrown in. It didn't seem like much until I filled out the tracking form and realized I was spending $74 a month (5 hours of my time!) for something that wasn't even that important to me. Besides that, I could drink coffee at work... for free! I then canceled an online service I no longer needed and was still paying $21 a month for. I had the cable company drop the landline I had never used after a free trial period, at $20 a month. I called my insurance agent and had them change my coverage to PLPD on my 2001 vehicle (2nd car), saving $30 a month. I then contacted HR at my place of employment and had them raise my deductions which gave me a whopping $80 extra a month. The tradeoff being, I wouldn't receive that big refund check in the spring, but I realized I needed to put that money to work (seek the advice of an accountant first-you don't want to be surprised and find you owe taxes at the end of the year). Within less than an hour I had found an extra $225. I now had $625 in monthly cash flow without making any significant sacrifices or changes to my current lifestyle. And, I didn't have to sell my kids!

One thing that had changed was how differently I began to see my discretionary spending. I now found myself asking, "how much time will I have to trade in order to cover this purchase?" Interestingly, 9 times out of 10, I would walk away... and, with a smile. I felt the "employee mentality" that had been holding me back for so long, beginning to loosen its grip. The desire to free myself of the living paycheck-to-paycheck life kept me vigilant, and on track. You can find some additional ways I found to watch my dimes in Chapter 9.

3) Identifying Debts Owed - Monthly Debt Target

In this step, identify each of your monthly debts owed and the cost associated with it. The Monthly Debt Target is where you list each debt, the minimum monthly payment, the interest you are paying, and the balance owed on the debt. Once you have all these figures, you will be better able to identify the most important accounts to target and in an order that will best benefit your financial position (freeing up that extra cash flow).

Everyone's situation is going to be different, however, the focus should be on the accounts that have the highest cost associated with it and free up cash flow the quickest.

On the following page I have listed the target debts I had when I started my journey (figures are rounded off to make the math easier to understand):

Monthly Debt Target

DEBT	PAYMENT	DUE DATE	BALANCE INTEREST RATE
Capital	325.00	24th	4,600 16%
Chase	40.00	28th	3,600 0%
Citibank	50.00	5th	2,300 0%
Penney	140.00	23rd	3,700 27%
Depot	71.00	3rd	2,300 22%
Student	158.00	16th	8,000 7%
Total	784.00		24,500

4) Choosing the line of credit (debt weapon)

As previously stated, velocity banking requires the use of a line of credit (LOC). It is important to be able to distinguish the difference between a LOC and a "loan." A LOC works with velocity banking because it is *revolving*, it is liquid, it allows the borrower to spend money, repay it, and spend it again; as opposed to taking out a "loan," which is close ended. When you make a payment on a loan, you no longer have access to that payment (money) you just made.

The LOC can be either secured or unsecured, e.g., home equity line of credit (HELOC), personal line of credit (PLOC), insurance policy, 401K, or even a credit card. Because of my poor debt-to-income ratio, I knew I would not be able to qualify for new lines of credit and I didn't have an insurance policy or 401K to borrow against. My LOC was a simple credit card (CC). If the LOC is revolving it will work with this strategy.

I had several credit cards, but decided to use my Capital One Visa because of its high limit of $10,000 along with a relatively low interest rate. The problem was, when I started the strategy, the card already had a $4,600 balance. I had a small savings (sitting unemployed) and with my new mindset, I wanted to put it to work. I deposited those funds ($800), into my CC lowering the balance to $3800. It wasn't easy letting go of that safety net, but I understood the funds were *still* at my disposal (through the revolving CC) so I felt secure in the decision. That's where I believe most people become nervous about the process. You must remember, when you put your available funds toward your LOC, they are still available for your use. You have not changed your financial position. You have just transferred your available liquidity to another vehicle. In the process, you have also decreased accruing interest. Again, you have no business keeping a savings account when you are in debt!

Although it wasn't necessary, I wanted to pay down my CC completely before I started with the velocity banking strategy. The main reason being, I wanted to make sure my cash flow prediction was on point and more importantly, I wanted to prove to myself I could follow through. With so many past failures to get out of debt, I wanted to be sure I could at least pay off this one card before starting.

Mission accomplished! With a cash flow of $625, it took me approximately 6 months to pay off my CC completely. Because I was now hyper-aware of my *time's* worth, I miraculously became a savvy spender and stopped purchasing unneeded liabilities. I now had a LOC with $10,000 of available credit to begin using the strategy of velocity banking. I was extremely focused and ready to begin.

5) Your New Checking

This step will be hard for some to grasp, understandably because it's not how we have been *groomed* to handle our paychecks. Your LOC is now your "new" checking/savings account. All your monthly income will go directly into the LOC, and all your monthly expenses will be paid from the LOC. Some of these lines have the convenience of check writing, which is an advantage since not all bills can be paid by CC. If you must begin with a CC, as I did, it can still serve as your new checking

23

account until you are in a better financial position to apply for a PLOC or a HELOC from your bank.

Unfortunately, I could not pay my mortgage, student loan or the other CCs using my LOC (CC). Since those bills had to be paid separately, I had to subtract those amounts needed to satisfy the monthly minimum payments and then deposit the rest into my CC. It is a slight inconvenience, but it is doable. There are ways around this, such as cash advances or with companies such as Plastiq, but it is hard to justify the amount they charge in fees. I have also heard of people using their PayPal business account to send an invoice to themselves and then pay the invoice through their CC. The payment received into their account is then used to pay bills that can't be paid by CC.

Every other expense that can be paid by CC should be paid from this account, such as: gas, groceries, cable, telephone, utilities, garbage, household supplies, laundry, subscriptions, entertainment, home repair, and miscellaneous needs. Make sure to keep a close eye on your expenses as the month progresses. It is very important to make sure your predicted cash flow remains on track. Remember, it's all about the cash flow!

6) On Your Mark, Get Set, Go

Once you have your ducks in a row, budget in hand and LOC established, it is now time to begin your attack using the velocity banking strategy!

Chapter 5

Chunking Calculations

The term "chunking" is the amount (sizable amount of cash) you will use from your LOC to pay toward a targeted debt in order to rapidly pay down the balance. The calculation used to determine the chunking amount should (to be conservative) be equal to 6 months of your predicted cash flow. Meaning that it will take you at least 6 months to pay back your LOC for the initial chunk payment. Do not make a chunk payment for the full amount from your LOC. This will provide you with a safety net (previously your savings) for life's unforeseen expenses and emergencies.

Personal Example

In my case, the calculations were 6 (months) x $625 (cash flow) = $3,750 (chunk payment). The first chunk was being used to pay off the highest credit card, JCPenney with a 27% interest rate, the balance at $3,550, down from the continuing payments. I also had to account for a $113 cash advance fee, another drawback of using a CC, but still worth the overall saving benefits. The remaining $200 went against my next highest interest target, the Home Depot card.

With that first chunk, I was able to increase my monthly cash flow by $140. I, then, began the process of paying down that balance on my LOC of $3,863 ($3,750 + $113 cash advance fee). With my new monthly cash flow of $765, this was accomplished in less than 5 1/2 months.

It was time for round two! I followed the same process by calculating the next chunk, but this time with my new cash flow amount, 6 (months) x $765 (cash flow) = $4590 (chunk payment). That chunk was used to pay off Home Depot and the rest towards the next debt in line. I followed this same process, over and over, until all four CCs were paid off. And then, after just 18 months, the final target, my student loan, finally received the "paid-in-full" stamp. With my cash flow now at $1,084, the LOC was paid back in less than 4 months. With that original LOC payment of $325, my total cash flow was now $1,409.

The Bottom Line

In just 22 months, I was able to pay off $24,500 in debt, raise my FICO score by more than 100 points, and increase my monthly cash flow by $1009! The amazing part was that I did it without increasing my income and I didn't have to survive on Ramen Noodles (although, I think they're yummy). I'm still amazed I was able to pay off that amount, within that time frame, starting with just $400 in monthly cash flow. I'm quite sure I would not have been able to duplicate those results by simply making an extra payment (whenever I had extra cash) because I would have *never* had extra cash!

The debt reduction strategy greatly improved my debt-to-income ratios and with a higher FICO score I was able to get approved for a $15,000 Personal Line of Credit (PLOC) from my bank. The PLOC is what I am currently using to target and accelerate my mortgage loan. I'm looking to knock off at least 10 years and approximately $54,000 in interest. Understanding the difference of how simple interest and amortized interest are calculated will help you to better understand how a LOC works to accelerate and save massive amounts of interest on mortgage loans.

No matter what debt reduction strategy you choose to follow, it will take time, discipline, and determination. For me, velocity banking was the missing piece of the puzzle. The strategy not only taught me the power of cash flow, but also how to leverage the *bank's* money to pay off *bank* debts. It also helped me to recognize the "employee mentality" that had me trapped in the paycheck-to-paycheck world. Knowledge is power, and once you grasp the concept of leveraging OPM and the downfalls of living in the "employee mindset," your view regarding your finances will forever be changed.

Chapter 6

Mortgage Attack

With finances in check, you are now in a place where you can focus on one of the biggest debts you will likely incur during your lifetime, your mortgage. Using the velocity banking method to starve off this interest is what I like to call the "icing on the cake."

The same principles used for attacking the interest payments on previous debts are used for shaving years and interest off mortgages.

Just imagine paying off that 30-year mortgage in as little as 5-9 years! Heck, if I only was able to shave 10-15 years off, I would be ecstatic. It would be like winning the lottery.

Remember, when using velocity banking strategies, you don't have to work a second or third job for extra income. You don't have to slash your spending habits or live on a strict budget. All you must do is change the way you bank! That's it.

Example: A $150,000 mortgage (30-year) at 6% will have payments of around $900. If you were to make just one extra $900 payment a year you would take close to **6 years** off your mortgage, saving approximately $38,000 in interest!

Now, if your debt is under control and you can make larger chunks, let's say $12,000 every 12 months, you would take close to 22 years off your mortgage, saving approximately $136,000 in interest. That's almost a whole other mortgage!

Note: Check with your mortgage company first. Some companies only accept extra payments at specific times or may charge prepayment penalties.

When making chunk payments *always* include a note on your extra payment that you want applied to the principal balance— not to the following month or several month's out payments.

Chapter 7

Okay, Now What?

Disclaimer: I am not a financial planner or expert in financial investing. The following are my experiences and opinions only.

Congratulations! You are debt-free and have successfully increased your monthly cash flow... now what? Until this point, everything we have focused on has pertained to eliminating debt, but that is just the beginning. Unless you are content to continue trading time for money, your next step is to educate yourself and set goals for financial freedom: acquiring and creating assets that will pay your expenses and liabilities. We're not looking for paycheck income but looking to generate passive income that can provide true financial freedom.

Investing in the market and real estate seem to be the two most popular routes used for achieving financial goals, but there are many other avenues available to us. Many people have dreams of owning their own businesses (home-based, or brick and mortar) whether it be restaurant, construction, daycare, accounting, clothing, MLM, online... as you can imagine, hundreds of thousands of options. Depending on your interests and talents, passive and residual income can be derived from writing, art, photography, music... also, a list that is virtually endless. Experimenting and working at "side gigs" outside your paycheck job have been known to take on a life of their own and are often used as a launching pad into other income producing opportunities. If you are unsure of your next step, it is best to continue "trading time for money" while you research and educate yourself on the options that interest you.

Writing is a passion of mine that has naturally evolved into a side gig. I have authored and self-published four children's picture books, but because I cannot live off the sales ($40-$80 a month), I continue to trade my time for money. One of my financial goals, while I continue my love of writing, is to increase sales that will eventually cover my expenses and liabilities.

Real estate is another area of interest. There are so many avenues when it comes to real estate investing, but I am most drawn to rentals and possibly the rent-to-own market. My goal, at this point, is to continue educating myself by reading and learning as much as I can from investors that have successfully built their wealth using this platform. Thanks to the velocity banking strategy, I feel I have the tools to leverage OPM and quickly pay down these types of investments to further increase cash flow.

I hesitate to make any long-term goals in real estate, but I have journaled the desire to have a few rental properties under my belt in the next five years. Your goals will forever be evolving and changing... as does life. I'm sure what was important to you five years ago is very different from what is important to you today.

Chapter 8

Journaling and Goal Setting

In life, you can either be a part of someone else's plan, or you can be a part of your own plan. The choice is easy. Journaling is a great tool for establishing accountability. Keeping a financial journal can help you set and achieve goals, monitor progress, see your weaknesses, make you more mindful of spending habits and most importantly... relieve stress! Journaling is not just for setting short and long-term financial goals, but can also help with to-do lists, ideas, thoughts, feelings, or anything that propels you in a positive way toward financial freedom. Whether you use it to plan, check-in, revise, delete or rewrite, by writing it down, you begin the process of creation. Remember, there is no right or wrong to journaling. Everyone's financial goals are different, and the paths to reach them vary greatly. Journaling is a great way to map out and plan your desired path.

Setting goals through journaling seems like a no-brainer to me now, but it hasn't always been a practice of mine. Looking back, I put more time and thought into planning my itinerary for a one-week vacation than I had in planning my life's journey. I believe this was because I hadn't spent enough time thinking about what I wanted out of life. I had just been following whatever path had been laid before me (mostly influenced by others). Seems silly to me now. After all, would anyone really set out on a major journey with no real idea of their destination? Probably not!

Through journaling, I now set marketing goals for my writing that involve social media, website development, author contests, writer's clubs, school readings, and continued education. I find that journaling increases awareness of my day-to-day time management as well as my financial mindset. Whenever I wander off-track, which I often do, revisiting my goal journal puts me right back in the game. My journal is my personal GPS. Putting pen to paper will not only help you to sort and clarify your goals, but it will keep you moving forward. The one common thread you will find in any successful person is their journaling (goal setting) habits.

Some of my favorite quotes on journaling and goal setting:

"The best way to predict your future is to create it." – Abraham Lincoln

"Setting goals is the first step in turning the invisible into the visible." – Tony Robbins

"People with goals succeed because they know where they're going." – Earl Nightingale

"Never go to sleep without a request to your subconscious." – Thomas Edison

"Goals allow you to control the direction of change in your favor." – Brian Tracy

"The No. 1 reason people fail in life is because they listen to their friends, family, and neighbors." – Napoleon Hill

Chapter 9

Common Concerns or Arguments

I don't want to close my checking and savings. I've had them forever.

You don't have to. Your paycheck still gets deposited into your checking or savings accounts, but now we just pass it through. Consider those accounts as transitional. Remember, the longer the money sits in checking and savings, the longer it remains unemployed (which is what the bank wants).

I need my savings. What if something happens or there's an emergency?

The money, previously sitting idle in your savings, is still available for your use. Only now, it is available from your LOC.

Why can't I just make extra payments towards my student loan. Wouldn't I get the same results?

You would have great results if you were able to do that on a consistent basis. The problem is most people don't follow through. They might set out with the best of intentions, but when it comes down to parting with that extra money, they psychologically can't do it. Another reason, once they make that extra payment, that money is gone. You can't swipe your student loan to pay for gas or groceries if you need it (remember once it's paid, it is no longer available to you). Now, if you were using a LOC, which is continually revolving, that money is still available.

Why would I use a LOC with a higher (16%) interest rate to pay off my student loan with a lower (7%) interest rate?

It's all about how the interest is calculated. With a LOC, the interest is calculated daily, and you only pay interest on the money you're using. Student loans, mortgages, and even some car loans are amortized with interest calculated on the total amount borrowed and a predetermined length of time. At the beginning of an amortized loan, interest costs are at their highest. Especially with long-term loans, most of each payment you make is interest, with very little toward the principal. In other words, you don't make much progress on the debt's principal amount during the early years. That's why "chunking" payments help to jump you forward on the amortized loan schedule to get to that principal sooner. The cost of a LOC pales in comparison to the amount of interest saved on an amortized loan when you can make those types of chunks.

Isn't this the same as the "debt snowball" method I've heard about?

The understanding of how interest and various debt vehicles charge interest can be so complex that some prefer methods like a "debt snowball" as it sets a simple plan to relieve debt. The strategy has worked well for many. With the debt snowball method, you list your debts in order of their balances and begin by throwing all your extra income towards the debt with the smallest balance while continuing to make the minimum on the others. After you get that first debt paid off you move your focus, and increased cash flow, toward the next debt in line. I tried this method several times, but as I stated earlier, I had a very hard time parting with any extra cash I had saved. Using the velocity banking strategy works for me because I always have access to my cash through the LOC.

Chapter 10

25 Ways to Save Your Dime

Although it is suggested to have at least $500 in monthly cash flow when beginning the velocity banking strategy, the more money you can free up, the quicker the strategy will get you to your financial goals. The following is a list of money-saving suggestions to help you in your quest. Many of these tips will seem familiar, but it doesn't hurt to revisit them. Hopefully, they will trigger further ways to help you in saving a dime. Remember, those dimes add up.

1. Tracking your variable expenses. I know, *here we go again!* Tracking is mentioned often because of its importance. I guarantee, if you carefully track your spending for a month, you will be surprised where your hard-earned money has been disappearing. Besides that, you will finally be able to answer the age-old question, "Where does it all go?"

2. Reach out to creditors. Call every creditor on your list to see if you can get a better deal, whether it be a better interest rate or the cost of service. It will take some time, but it might be worth it. With all the competition out there, many companies are more than happy to help, in order to keep you as a customer.

3. Automated payments. A lot of creditors will give you a small discount if you set up automatic payments with them. Both my mortgage and car insurance payments offer a slight percentage discount by using this convenience. It never hurts to check.

4. Question yourself. This one tip helped me tremendously. Before you make a purchase, first ask yourself the question; *How much of my time will I need to trade in order to possess this?* Instead of looking at price tags, I began looking at "time tags." Asking myself the question truly made a difference when it came to my spending. Another question I began to ask myself; *Is this a need or a want?* It's almost always a "want." It's so much easier to walk away when you answer these questions honestly.

5. Shop around and compare insurance prices. Even if it's only a $50 savings, it adds up. You can also play around raising your deductibles to save some money. If you can't find a lower quote, at least you'll know you're getting the best bang for your buck.

6. Check your W-4 and see if the deductions you are claiming can be changed to free up monthly cash flow. Make sure to do your due diligence. You do not want to be surprised with a big tax bill at the end of the year. Forget about that tax refund in the spring. You need to put that money to work for you now.

7. Stop the fancy coffees! I can't scream this loud enough... sorry Starbucks. A $5-6 coffee, 5 days a week adds up to more than $1,300 a year! How many hours do you have to work to enjoy that cup of Joe? I realized I was working 7+ hours a month to pay for my ridiculous splurge. Coffee at your local grocery store is pennies in comparison. You can buy a large brand-name can of coffee for less than $7 that brews 240 cups of coffee. Get

creative. Google recipes. I bet you can easily duplicate that "special" coffee drink at a fraction of the amount you are paying. Sure, it's more convenient, but remember, we're in a debt-paying mode.

8. Bottled water. I've never understood this H2O fad. It has been reported that the cost of bottled water is 2000 times that of water from our tap! Americans spend 12 billion dollars a year on bottled water. Can we really be that crazy? I once listen to a doctor from a middle eastern country who was puzzled with America's obsession with bottled water. He goes on to describe their country's scorching temperatures, and yet you never see their citizens walking around with designer water brands in hand. Are we just spoiled, or have we just fallen into another advertising trap of "must haves?" I think we can do better. An estimated 45% of water found in grocery store aisles is the same as what you get from taps. Get a filter if you want it to be purified. Slice some lemon to give it some pizzazz. Put it in gallon jugs and keep it in your refrigerator. Take a jug to work or pour it into reusable bottles for a quick grab-n-go; heck, drink it out of crystal goblets if it makes you feel better. Our environment will thank you!

9. Try coloring your hair at home. It's not as scary as you might think. I mentioned to my hairdresser that I was trying to save some money and she told me exactly what I needed to buy to color my hair at home between haircuts. This alone has saved me at least $250 a year. I've also stretched out the times in between visits, which has helped to save additional dollars.

10. Packing lunch. If you normally go out for lunch, this can save you a lot. You don't have to do it every day. Start out with one or

two days a week. I can't think of a better way to use up leftovers, and it would probably be a lot healthier for you.

11. Preparing snacks ahead. If you have children or grandchildren, you know the importance of snacks. Whether going to a school event, sporting event, park, zoo, or playground, make sure to prepare those all-important snacks and drinks. The trick is being creative and fun, so no one will feel they are missing out. This will keep you from having to visit the concession stand.

12. Turn down your thermostat. Okay, I can see you rolling your eyes. It seems obvious, but many times, this tip is overlooked. One degree higher or lower, depending on the season, will make a difference. Try two degrees, if you're daring. I'm sure this one move needs no further explanation.

13. Shut the lights off. Another "duh" tip. One phrase I continually heard growing up, "When you leave a room, shut the lights off; money doesn't grow on trees!" You would have thought I'd learned my lesson by now. To some extent, I did, but I know I could do better. As I look around the house right now, the kitchen light is on... and I'm not in the kitchen.

14. Couponing. I've never been a "couponer." I hated the time it took to find them, cut them out, then plan where I had to shop to redeem them for the best value. I was always kicking myself at checkout, after realizing I left them in the car, or worse, at home on the counter. When I finally remembered to bring them, they were either expired or else I purchased the 12 Oz cereal, and the coupon was only good on the 14 Oz box. I just didn't have the time to play with them. I've since learned that they can

be a very valuable savings. Like everything else, planning and organization can save you lots of time and money.

15. Online subscriptions. Are you using the ones you thought you could not live without? I loved the Skillshare.com site. I learned a lot in the first week I had it. Three months later, not so much. Not that I didn't like, or want, what the site offered, I just wasn't using it like I thought I would. Same with Netflix. I loved the fact that it was there if I had the whim to binge-watch on a Sunday afternoon, but I couldn't remember the last time I did. Plus, I was already paying for cable that boasted 300 different channels. How much television could a person watch anyway? Those are the types of subscriptions you need to look at. Cancelling Skillshare saved me $21, and Netflix saved another $19.99.

16. Phone plans. I knew I couldn't do much better regarding my phone plan. I have been with the same prepaid phone carrier for 10 years. I pay $45 a month for unlimited text, calls, and data for my android phone and have had absolutely no complaints. My sister, on the other hand, not only pays double for her fancy iPhones, but also for her service. I've never understood this. My phone and service have the exact same capabilities as hers. Why would anyone in their right mind pay more? Again, shop around.

17. Share garbage service. I used to do this with my previous neighbor. Between us, we only had one or two bags of garbage to dispose of in a week. The garbage service allowed for six, so our garbage bill was cut in half.

18. Wash your laundry in cold water. Unless you are laundering cloth diapers, there is very little need for you to wash your duds in hot water. Your clothes will not only last longer, but your energy bill will be lowered.

19. Weekly meal planning. Taking the time to plan your menu for the entire week is not only a time saver, but also a big money saver. Knowing exactly what is needed will keep you from having to make several trips to the grocery store and ensure you will not just be throwing unneeded items in the cart. The grocery store is filled with temptations. Stick to your list! Meal planning will also help in utilizing the leftovers for the next day's lunches.

20. Instead of socializing at a bar or a club, invite friends over to your place. My friends were aware I was trying to cut back, so they had no problem with our patio socials. These BYOB gatherings became a big hit. Just throw out a box of crackers and some cheese slices and everyone's a happy camper.

21. Experiment with generic brands at the grocery store. When it comes to generics, there are some you will have a hard time telling from the name brands. On the other hand, there are some generics you can't even convince your dog to eat. It doesn't hurt to experiment. There can be some big savings there.

neric drugs. I can't remember the last time I bought a ame acetaminophen or ibuprofen. The only way that rands differ from the brand names is their impact on ot your body. Check the labels and compare osages.

23. Drive-thru car wash. Although I occasionally pay $8 for the convenience ($9 if you include the tip), there is no reason I can't wash my own car in the driveway. Besides, my grandchildren love to help, and I always feel so much better afterward.

24. Thrift stores. I have a daughter who absolutely loves thrift shopping. I reluctantly tagged along one day, and I quickly changed my tune about thrifting. I happened to come across a pair of Sketchers in my size that looked as if they'd never been worn, with a $5 price sticker! It so happened I needed a pair for work. I had been looking online and knew I couldn't get that exact shoe for less than $85. Yes, you do have to spend some time searching through a jungle of racks, but a hit like that, kept $80 in my back pocket.

25. One of America's favorite treats, ice cream! During the summer months, we visited our local ice cream parlor more times than I could count. Recently, I have learned that children don't care where they get the ice cream from, if you make it fun. For the price of one banana split at the local Cone Zone, I can get a half gallon of ice cream and a few bananas to feed us all. Of course, grandma always has a stash of fun toppings on hand. Top them off with a dollop of whipped cream and everyone's a happy camper. Believe me; you won't feel deprived with this money-saving hack.

Chapter 11

Final Tips for Success

Don't be your worst enemy. You need to be *brutally* honest when filling out your Monthly Tracking Form. The more meticulous you are about what is coming in and going out each month, the quicker the strategy will work.

Continually look for places to "plug holes" to increase monthly cash flow.

Do not forget to account for life events; Christmas, birthdays, any other upcoming situations you know will have an impact on that particular month.

Respect your LOC! Use *only* for the expenses you have previously allocated in your Monthly Income/Expense Statement. Your LOC is not meant to be used to purchase "more liabilities" which will quickly drive you off course in reducing debt.

Be conscious when making purchases, first ask yourself *"How much of my time will I need to trade in order to possess this?"* As in my revelation with my daily frappe splurges. Were they worth the 5 hours I would have to work each month? For me, absolutely not! The most valuable asset on this planet is "time." Once it is lost, it can never be replaced.

Becoming debt-free is only the first step to becoming financially independent. Acquiring income producing assets to cover your expenses should be the final goal so that you can live the life that you choose.

Knowledge is power. Never quit educating yourself.

Journal, Journal, Journal. There is a reason that keeping a journal is a common habit of successful people.

Chapter 12

Sample of Velocity Tracking Forms I used

MONTHLY VARIABLE SPENDING

VB MONTHLY TRACKER

Use this form to track your variable expenses for the month. Fill in empty spaces to suit your needs.

FOOD	GAS	FUN	CLOTHES				Miscellaneous

The first step (in my opinion, the most important) is the monthly variable spending tracker. Variable expenses are costs that fluctuate from month to month. Some examples of variable expenses include groceries, gas, entertainment, haircare, beauty products, prescriptions, vacations, clothing, holiday spending, hobbies, etc.

If you are serious about getting a handle on debt, it's important to track every penny you spend on your variable expenses for at least one month. Have a tracker easily assessable and record every penny you spend, no matter how small or whether you pay in cash, debit, or credit. If you share finances with a partner, it's imperative to make sure they are on board with the same commitment. I promise you; this will be an eye-opener.

Most of us have a general idea of where our money is going each month, but the "pennies" seem to get lost in the big picture as we juggle our day-to-day lives with work, family, and other obligations. Those "pennies" matter!

I immediately felt empowered after taking this proactive approach of tracking. If you recall, this is where I realized my daily $3 coffee stops were adding up to more than $80 each month! It might not seem like a lot for some, but I quickly realized I had to work at least **five** hours (trading my time) to pay for something that I easily could live without. Especially because I could get coffee at no cost at work. Obviously, the coffee no longer held the same value under those trade terms!

Tracking pivoted my way of thinking.

I found myself dissecting *every* purchase. My decisions were no longer made by price or want, but by how long I had to work (trade my time) to obtain whatever it was.

MONTHLY INCOME/DEBT

Monthly Personal Budget Worksheet

	Estimated Monthly Cost	x 12
INCOME		
Income (Draw) From Business	$ _____	$ _____
Income From Other Sources	$ _____	$ _____
TOTAL INCOME	$ _____	$ _____
EXPENSES		
Rent/Mortgage	$ _____	$ _____
Home Insurance	$ _____	$ _____
Health Insurance	$ _____	$ _____
Utilities	$ _____	$ _____
Telephone	$ _____	$ _____
Auto: (payments, gas, repairs)	$ _____	$ _____
Food	$ _____	$ _____
Household Supplies	$ _____	$ _____
Clothing	$ _____	$ _____
Laundry/Dry Cleaning	$ _____	$ _____
Education	$ _____	$ _____
Entertainment	$ _____	$ _____
Travel	$ _____	$ _____
Contributions	$ _____	$ _____
Health	$ _____	$ _____
Home Repair and Maintenance	$ _____	$ _____
Self-Development	$ _____	$ _____
Outstanding Loans and Credit Card Payments	$ _____	$ _____
Miscellaneous Expenses	$ _____	$ _____
TOTAL EXPENSES	$ _____	$ _____
BALANCE (+/-)	$ _____	$ _____

After tracking variable expenses it's time to record your monthly income (everything coming in) and your monthly fixed expenses (everything going out).

Most people have a good grasp on what their income is each month.

Of course, this depends on your line of work, but the closer you can get to those numbers the better.

Fixed expenses are a little easier to track; mortgage, insurance, taxes, loan payments, cable, garbage, phone, all of which are expected in your budget.

The Income/Debt Tracker totals monthly totals and yearly figures.

If you want to use the Velocity Banking Strategy to reduce your debt, you need to have at least a surplus of $500 a month. This might seem impossible for some. Don't be discouraged. I was in the same boat, and I encourage you to take it as a challenge.

Find the money!

MONTHLY DEBT TARGETS

Debt Owed	Payment Amount	Due Date	Balance	Interest Rate

Monthly Debt Targets

Targeting your monthly debt is the final proactive step to tackling your debt head on. I must admit, I was shocked after I had everything down on paper. I was embarrassed but have since realized I am not alone. Most people you ask will have no idea what the rates are on their borrowed money and sadly, I was one of them.

I went through everything down to the penny. At this point I was so angry with myself; I was determined to get myself out of this money trap.

Whether using the *Avalanche* method (tackling highest interest first) or the *Snowball* method (tackling lowest balances first) this step will give you a view of the damage and where you need to start.

Remember, whatever method works for you, is the RIGHT method for you!

A Word from the Author

This short read was born purely out of my desire to help explain velocity banking to my adult children. Every time I tried to discuss the concept, they either became lost in my explanation, or were too stubborn to except there could be a more efficient way to pay off debt. After witnessing how quickly I was able to become debt free, they increasingly became more open to learning about velocity banking strategies.

Over the last several years, all four of my children have achieved the American dream of owning a home. With the knowledge they have learned while using these strategies, they continue to use the bank's own secrets to tackle their mortgages. Once you know, you know.

I cannot describe to you how excited I am to see velocity banking working for them. I only wish I had learned of the strategies when I was first starting out. The information I have uncovered was just too good not to share with others looking to find their way out of the debt trap.

FREEBIES

Sign up for my newsletter and receive FREE copies of the forms I use for setting financial goals and tracking progress.

☐ Monthly Tracker

☐ Monthly Income/Expense Form

☐ Debt Targets

To receive your FREE downloads of debt reduction forms email charlienichols_author@yahoo.com

Final Thoughts

Millions of people have bought into a life of trading their time for money, it's a vicious hamster wheel and we pass our ignorance of how money works down generation to generation. There are many lessons we teach our children in life, but I believe we come up short when it comes to money and finance, mostly because we were never taught the basics ourselves.

I wish you the very best at achieving your goals. It's hard to enjoy the little things in life when you're constantly thinking about debt. I truly hope this book has brought some hope and inspiration in your quest to be debt free.

Knowledge is power and it's never too late to learn.

Velocity Banking Notes

_____

_____

_____

_____

_____

_____

_____

_____

_____

_____

_____

_____

_____

_____

_____

_____

_____

_____

_____

Printed in the USA
CPSIA information can be obtained
at www.ICGtesting.com
LVHW031119050624
782326LV00006B/121